# Crossing
# Over

For DeWitt Henry —
With Thanks For
Setting This
Book In Motion —

Richard Currey
7/15/93

# Crossing Over

The Vietnam
Stories

# Richard Currey

CLARK CITY PRESS
LIVINGSTON, MONTANA

LIBRARY OF CONGRESS CATALOGING-IN-PUBLICATION DATA
CURREY, RICHARD, 1949–
    CROSSING OVER : THE VIETNAM STORIES / RICHARD CURREY.
    P. CM.
    ISBN 0-944439-21-7
    1. VIETNAMESE CONFLICT, 1961–1975 — LITERARY COLLECTIONS.
I. TITLE.
PS3553.U6665C75    1993
813'.54 — dc20                                        92-32124
                                                        CIP


AN EXCERPT OF THIS BOOK ORIGINALLY APPEARED,
IN A DIFFERENT FORM, IN *WITNESS*, 1991.



CLARK CITY PRESS
POST OFFICE BOX 1358
LIVINGSTON, MONTANA 59047

CLARK CITY PRESS publishes handsome books by fine writers and artists, covering fiction to photography, mysteries to memoirs, essays to poetry. All our editions are printed on acid-free paper and most have sewn bindings. If you would like to be on our mailing list, please complete this card or call us at (800) 835-0814.

_____
*Name*

_____
*Street*

_____
*City*                              *State*      *Zip*

_____
*Title of the book in which you found this card*

_____
*How did you hear about this book?*

I am particularly interested in:

☐ Fiction                    ☐ Poetry

☐ Art/Photography            ☐ Nature/Sporting

☐ Essays/Memoirs             ☐ Limited Editions

CLARK CITY PRESS

POST OFFICE BOX 1358

LIVINGSTON, MT  59047

FOR THE KINDRED

# Author's Note

In 1980, my first book was published, a collection of poems and prose poems entitled *Crossing Over: A Vietnam Journal*. That book carried about half the actual manuscript I was then working on, but with time and other projects and a life moving rapidly in various directions the unpublished portion of *Crossing Over* was misplaced. It was not until the summer of 1991 that I unexpectedly recovered the lost pages, and began thinking about a new edition that would finally include the long-missing pieces. Happily, Clark City Press was interested in publishing such an edition.

My plan was to simply incorporate the lost sections into the original manuscript, but when I sat down with the material I found myself again in the grip of the war itself, inside the fields of memory, interacting with words I'd put on paper as long ago as 1972. The result is that fully half of this book is entirely new. It is *Crossing Over*, but a revised and revived version, a fresh account. It is a palpably different work from its namesake, reflecting not only my sense of these vignettes as stories—with each section serving as a chapter of a single narrative—but the long and hard shadow that Vietnam has continued to cast in my generation's life.

*I passed my first days in-country watching rain from the doorways of a warehouse full of displaced marines. We were the soldiers clocking in—fresh uniforms, fresh haircuts, clean shaves, clean boots, gleaming weapons. Every morning and afternoon I waited in lines, waiting for a way north to the combat unit I had been assigned to. Everybody I talked with affected a stance: boredom, preoccupation, cavalier disdain, stand-up comic hilarity. There was an emptiness of eyes and one marine who muttered* fortunes of war, fortunes of war *in response to anything he was asked or told. In time I flew north to join my unit, on operations in the bush. The first few weeks in the field were uneventful. I was told it was usually this way—and then the sky reached down to eat you alive. The first enemy contact was at night, a frontal assault on our position. I was thrown onto my back in a gully by the marine next to me and watched the tracer rounds trade back and forth over my head, white, blue, fiery orange. There was a grenade explosion, and the incident was over. My platoon rose slowly, one at a time into the smoking night until I was the only man still on the ground, lying on my back in the dirt. The entire episode lasted ninety seconds, perhaps two minutes. Probably nothing more than enemy fire teams surprised by each other, passing too closely in the jungle. The tracer rounds were beautiful, wild light, a kind of insane geometry of the air. I stood, and I was not afraid. Peculiar, and surprising: no cold sweat, no nauseating rip through the gut, no loss of bladder control, no adrenaline screech in the bloodstream. I stood in the gully and felt nothing. But that would change. I would not be spared: all of the body's failures were yet to come, and with each day I grew more frightened, more desperate, living on memory's pale motions in the dark and the relentless misery of truth.*

I

Maldonado in the ditch bottom whispering in Spanish, his blood mixing the rain, hands fluting the air like he's reaching for something flying that evades him. His leg gone at the thigh. I use his belt to tie off the stump.

The firefight pocks and talks above us. Maldonado looks at me, actually smiling and says Guess I stepped in some shit, right?

I 957. My grandfather was still healthy and we would visit. At the biggest department store in town a lunch counter flew a mural above it depicting the town from the air on one panel, the state-champion high-school marching band on the other. Waxed parquet floors, toys downstairs and to the right, the best selection of comic books in town. The girls that sold popcorn were modest teenagers with glasses, transistors under the counter: low-fidelity Five Satins, Ronettes, Roy Orbison.

The platoon's moved onto a cleared dike, just humping now. Motherfucker the radioman says through his teeth, cutting pace to fall in next to me, Who's this goddam Lieutenant think he is? We're up here like ducks.

I keep walking, don't answer. We're up here sitting for a goddam max the radioman says. Dinks take us out one at a goddam time. Be a motherfuckin turkey shoot.

U p and dancing.

Up and rolling water hips, arms tucked close to carry the drumming wrists, jungle boot ridged soles chipping the ridged lid of the ammo chest, Egyptian belly-dance chicken-neck strut, tough bitch Junior Walker two-step distorted from his cassette on the ground.

Shifting into basecamp. Soft canvas on metal or flesh. The patrol shapes in against trees, canteen ring, the usual. Everyone tried in his own way, mudslapped. The only one not into the music is the Lieutenant from Alabama. His responsibility to maintain an atmosphere where there's never dancing among grim men doing their duty at the front.

Cut that shit off the Lieutenant shouts across the area. But the song's already over.

The need to bear witness is basically what I'm into he says, taking six squares to Park Place. Guns in the distance, AK-47s beating a treeline, rattling like bolts in a Mason jar— somebody straddling the horizon, shadow of the figure against the clouds, shaking the ritual, moving shoulders slightly with the rhythm, talking to the sky: this is where we live. This is what we eat. This is what we hate.

I don't wanna buy it he says. But don't touch them die I threw doubles if you'll recall. He goes again, blowing into his closed hands, whispering, and tosses a one and a one. There it is Doc, he says. Snake eyes. The answer to the grunt's prayer. When I'm out in the boonies I always say my little prayer. Lord, gimme a pair of them dink snake eyes.

An encounter in deep jungle, an inconsequential encounter where the enemy is never seen and not one of our men is so much as scratched. Machine-gun fire erupts and we drop flat as the foliage above our heads is razored away and drifts over us, over our helmets, shoulders, backs. The Lieutenant crawls about, trying to position and direct; we answer the fire blindly, rocking bullets here and there into the brush. A brittle scream. It seemed to come from in front of us, but it is impossible to be sure. It might have been one of us, but we all look to be intact. A grenade thumps off to my right — empty territory. I cannot be sure if it was thrown at us, or from behind me; underbrush and tree limbs rip up into the lower canopy and shower away. Sergeant Halverson coordinates a fire team: their volley slices across ninety degrees of jungle at waist level, cutting down the smaller trees that waver and lean, hesitate, fall out of sight to the forest floor or slipping like drunks into the arms of the trees around them. And now there is no gunfire in response. Now the only sounds are the sounds of the forest. There is a nerve-end interference inside my ears, electrical, buzzing, and I know it's nothing except my own body attempting to stay in one place, in one piece. This encounter will be reported as enemy contact, although none of us could confirm beyond a doubt that we were not shooting at a friendly unit, Australians, South Vietnamese, other Americans. We could not even confirm that anything happened beyond some shared hallucination, beyond an exercise of our new and resolute belief in the unidentified and invisible, in the lyrical panic of ghosts. We continue to move into the shrouded light, one leg and another, slowly, parting leaves with rifle barrels as if a skeletal face will be there, suddenly inches away, waiting, smiling. This is the true beginning of our pain.

I think there will be constant sun. A long and awesome heat.

in, days of it. Skies
oles, sandbag em-
ce You don't have
s around here. Doc
ar? I grin, nod, say
e in a while. What
k, the need to keep
nind. Without such
shaking hands, the
a singular voice re-
ategorical precision,
nside my mouth and
of old water in the
tableaux of corpses
standing on the landscape like markers, directions, statements;
without the heavy work of humping or digging or the preoccupation of a firefight the past of every day is never past, always
in view and insisting on a particular version of the truth. Now
I dig, working into the sweat when a marine calls out that he's
found something and I move closer, seeing the bone. We
scrape around it and it is clearly a human bone, a leg bone, a
femur. Sergeant Halverson tries to lift it free of the mud, to
no avail. We dig around it and see it is held fast by its con-
nection to the bone above it, a hipbone flagged with decayed

strips of cloth. The spine is a splintered rift laid neatly in place, descending from the center of the ribcage. The ribs are fitted here and there with matted shreds of the same cloth that settled into the cavity of the pelvis, and a marine works around the sternum, the clavicle, the fragile white bird-bones of the neck, the hollowed fallen chin and gutted jaw. The face uncovers, Halverson pushing back mud until we see that the top of the skull is missing but the eyesockets below the brow are somehow intact. I get up and out to stand above and look down at the bones locked into the floor of the hole as if the ground had been carved for perfect fit. You know, Halverson says, like I told you, Doc. You don't need to do any of this kind of stuff. If you don't want. The fire team in the pit below us begins to tear out the bones, stacking them beside this trench it is our job to dig.

I recline nude on this bed that is too small. I turn my head and watch the second hand move. I am in the process of forgetting my name. A glittering church hovers above me and I remember an actor who called it a church of the heart and said the choir was on fire. In the pews various colorful beasts watch the blaze calmly. In the rear a very handsome gorilla and an Oriental prostitute have lit candles and dance sadly to the Victrola. I move in the aisles chanting Remember John Dillinger. Prairie fires. The Invention of Firearms. The Rise of Mussolini. Remember Burlesque in the twenties: who was that woman I saw you with last night? That was no woman, that was my knife. Remember the Lusitania. Yellow Fever. Those old postcards of leprosy in the Congo. Remember my uncle who showed around yellowed snapshots of the best friend he killed in a hunting accident in 1932. Maestro! Music please! My mother is about to dance the spotlight dance with a young man in uniform. Hats off please. I am in the process of forgetting my name.

After I graduated from high school and before I was drafted, I went to work in a warehouse. Roxanne worked in the accounting office and she was beautiful, a few years older, Mediterranean exotic, smooth and self-collected, centered. I watched her through the glass-wall partition of the accounting office, at her adding machine or typewriter, and imagined I wasn't being obvious, that I was subtle. On a day in late autumn Roxanne came back from lunch and walked straight at me until she was directly in front of me and said quietly I know you're in love with me. I was shocked and lost in the clarity of her stare and I stood there, submissive, absolutely in love with her. That afternoon my partner on the packing line said absently Hey man, you hear? Roxanne's boyfriend got it over in Nam. I looked at Curt, and he shrugged, wrenching tape around a crate. I guess she just got the news, he said. I pushed my crate off the belt and turned the conveyor off and looked toward Roxanne's window. She was typing, cool and mindful, earning the money but living somewhere else. I watched her steadily and she never looked up.

We lived in West Virginia when my father left for Korea. He explained his leaving to me gently, spoke about the war and my mother carefully, slowly. The week before he left there was a feathery tension and confusion, my mother constantly in tears. He gave me a tricycle for the sake of his disappearance and I rode it in his memory and with the energy of his anger. Then it rained, the run of days sounding in our lives like rain. At night, after midnight, steeple bells walked into the black air each hour and I dreamed I heard, or actually heard, trains hooting and passing miles off.

I try to dream about the past, calling it forward from what passes for sleep only to find it disappeared, as gone as blood hosed from a wall: the true heart of the forgotten. Where I am now, where I speak from, looks to any eye like paradise. The native home of the sun. The place where all of time's legends might have first entered the world and come to rest. In this paradise birds coalesce in flight, gush toward me and over my head and out to sea; on a street in a local city a policeman on his appointed rounds pistol-whips a woman in front of her terrified family. I walk on. The years pass in moments. Tides, waterfalls, the open arms of lightning. Here in paradise I am unable to fly, staring without comprehension at signs, faces, compasses. We can all deny failure as we embrace brutality, loving one as we hate the other, never believing in the single-mindedness of both, in the ruined honesty they carry, and I want nothing more than to say *Yes* to the moon, to the empty seas on its face like a tired man's crooked smile, *Yes* to the musical sweep of birds sliding across this perfect sky.

H ere are the facts of the matter.

    In 1964 President Lyndon Johnson used the perhaps spurious Gulf of Tonkin incident to promulgate a full-scale declaration of war against North Vietnam. The rest we know.

Here are the facts of the matter.

    On a combat operation with a Marine Corps unit, my platoon comes under fire. I use a U.S. Government standard-issue non-retractable ballpoint pen to open an airway for a marine shot in the face and unable to breathe in anything approaching a normal manner. This procedure is done by placing the pen a few centimeters below the cartilage in the lower neck and shoving it directly into the trachea. Having done this and established an at least temporarily patent airway I remove the pen and wipe it on my trouser leg and return it to my pocket in the event it should be necessary for any similar situation in the future.

Later that day I use the same pen for a short report and, that night, to complete the graves registration for two marines who died of their wounds in triage.

Rivers of men — columns, depots, terminals. Armies and navies in warehouses, a way that history paints itself: in terms of men shunted, shipped, airlifted, turned, streamed, paraded. Examined, assessed, directed, trained, reeducated. *You do solemnly swear to protect and defend the Constitution of the United States of America* double-time here, there, everywhere. Swamps and roads, America's last golden light in places rivers of men have never been and wish never to see again

the metallic sunrise of the virtuous prodded into view, the go-ahead, the green light, *by your leave, sir.* The snap of the Stars and Stripes alongside the regimental colors in an early brisk wind *enough to bring tears to your eyes.* Solace of a chest-high river like two hands against your breast and pushing: in another time, alone, you'd fish a river like this, you'd know the big fish are here, under the trees, in the dark, waiting to avoid you, a fine enemy. Rivers of men in storehouses, repositories, in formation, in lines, in rows, this face of history that is every face allowed its passing moment *here's your complimentary copy of "A Marine's Guide to the Republic of Vietnam" read it in good health.* A corps consists of two divisions, usually; a battalion consists of two companies, maybe more; a company consists of two platoons, usually; a platoon could have forty or so men on a good day think about cardiac tamponade, gentlemen, and what is that, exactly? It is when, secondary to invasive trauma or a good crashing blow to the chest wall there is bleeding around the lining of the heart obviously compromising the function of that most important organ. When you listen with a stethoscope you will find what the cardiologists call a "quiet heart." Watch for that sign, gentlemen, it's not all that uncommon in combat that's all for today thank you for your attention

rivers of men, waiting and dreaming, and I am one of the river, only one, afloat midstream, the sky wheeling overhead, destination unknown in a river we would fish in another time, a river that might support any number of families and probably has but now is only in the way and must be crossed and carries disease and hides the enemy on the other side and is no decent home for a quiet heart

*M*ontage: a few yellowed photographs of young crewcuts smiling together shirtless with rifles. On liberty in full-dress uniforms grinning in front of Bangkok whorehouse. Holding Batman comic books and *Playboy* magazines on display in lurid Polaroid color, leaning against a sun-glazed armored personnel carrier.

A song sung in the image, black-and-white photo creased in the singing: thin white man looking out of his face tired and on the verge, even smaller Vietnamese woman next to him, smiling primly in the attempt to delude.

In the long wake of sex I stare up into the violet. She has hung my old parachute over the ceiling. I jumped with it but it ripped, turning me back to the practice field breaking my ankle. I follow the sewn tear, remembering the sense of the fall. She feels me awake, moves her hand on my chest, talks again about my staying, in the Peace Corps or with the State Department or CIA, on the black market, anything. I am obsessed with tenderness and salvation and imagine the birds of her sleep aloft in the night's hidden skies. I am what I have lost, clocks running down in high corners of the room. She is the benevolence and redemption that confuses me when I love her. Taxicab headlamps draw color across the parachute air, the artillery pops distant, nearly fantasies. Tomorrow night I'll be airborne over her country, rose-stained bodies dumped in the chopper's gut, cartoon tracers of phantom ground fire blowing up toward us. Everyone will call me Doc as though it's a holy title, they'll clutch my arms as if I'm a christ. And when the night is over I'll sleepwalk, all over the country, out onto the Pacific, moving east and not opening my eyes for days.

I have been walking a long time. Everything about the forest is glazed and bizarre: trees hanging upside down with dark birds floating in the stark roots like fish. When I look at my feet they are huge and foreign, shapeless black oblongs that are connected to me but I cannot feel, that do not belong to me. The walking pads on, my head drifting weightless above the feet and legs and chest like a helium balloon towed in a parade. I keep feeling a fall is inevitable, a hole or precipice, and I try to stop but there is a distorted, sleepy inertia. The walking goes simply on and the boredom and odd silence collect like heavy fluids in my throat and behind my eyes: it is the kind of dream that runs down under its own gravity and I wake up quietly, cut loose and empty.

Feet over the edge and working my way down the bunks, four of them. My jungle boots unlaced and shuffling: I limp into the head, punch out a handful of water and rub my face. The glance in the mirror before going to a stall. I sit down and see somebody's taped up a picture of a woman fucking herself with a shiny green plastic dildo.

I get out before the fear works on me.

H ere are the facts of the matter.

Miguel Maldonado is nineteen years of age, a Lance Corporal in the United States Marine Corps, a first-generation Cuban-American from Miami, Florida. He is smart, funny, courageous. A high-school dropout who speaks with a strong Spanish accent, he is a former regional Golden Gloves finalist and holds the Purple Heart, the Bronze Star, and several unit commendations and battle stars. He has, on more than one occasion, saved the lives of his fellow marines and platoon commander. He gets on with everybody in his unit, no matter their backgrounds, prejudices, religion, or politics. He has a natural inclination toward excellence: a soldier's soldier. He speaks of a career in the Marine Corps, telling everyone he has found a home at last. He is astonished to find himself successful and, despite the stress of combat, he is a happy man. It is in the last days of 1968 that Maldonado loses his right leg at mid-thigh and I use his belt as a crude tourniquet in the minutes before he is airlifted to the Naval Hospital at Cam Ranh Bay. When I see him next it is by chance, having escorted two wounded marines into the same hospital. There has been some trouble with the leg—a sloppy amputation, an infection—and Maldonado is medically addicted to opiates of one form or another. The bright energy and wide-eyed courage are gone. Maldonado knows he has entered the next stage of his life: a disabled Cuban high-school dropout drug addict, without prospects or direction. I sit with him beside his bed. When I rise to go he grips my wrist. After a moment, however, he drops his hand. I say good-bye, wish him well, but he does not answer or look at me.

Here are the facts of the matter.

What we see and know will live forever in this snapping light in the eyes, the mouth shaping one question after another, the voice sounding one question after another, the piracy of time saying *I can go no further than this. It is unsafe to go further than this.* Flowing back into the blank hard eye of a soldier's one job, this last freedom failing into the heart, never fully knowing how far you can go if called to the task, how long the darkness is or how far above your head it extends, how long you might walk before the earth gives way in a watery lost moment, knowing the soldier's one job is not a complicated affair: locate the enemy and, having done so, destroy that enemy by any means available before the same intention is visited from the opposite direction. It is a game of sorts, a contest, winners taking nothing in this elaborate boy's contest taken to the limit of imagination and current possibility. Look around: the jungle sings. The insects and snakes and hardwoods breathe, and I can nearly believe they know we are here, sense our passage and find us ridiculous, transitory, at odds with existence, objects suitable only for pity. The sky reaches ground in patches, its weight giving root to the forest floor we cross, the forest a book we cannot read, legs moving against it, insect rattle, hollow monkey bone. I could conjure an entire magic out of this forest floor, braising dead leaves and mud between the palms, chanting under my breath *monkey bone take me home, take me home, take me home*

McCormick's face in the incoming's scream-whistle-crunch, his face in mine saying More guys in there I know there's more guys in there. We were coming into the perimeter, just outside the wire, heard the first scream and laid down flat, the world lit up and bounced. Gotta get em out McCormick says. You're not goin anywhere Sergeant Halverson shouts from my other side. Gotta get em to the Doc here McCormick shouts back. Make sense shitbrain Halverson says. Mac stands up and moves forward. I try to stand and stop him but Halverson two-fists the seat of my pants, knocking me down. Mac rolls under the wire, runs into blue-light clearing and pulls two men, lifting them up and under his arms like dolls. Holy fuckin christ Halverson says. One of the men Mac's carrying comes apart under his arm like rotten food and Mac keeps moving toward us. The other man is alive and gasping, groaning. OK Doc, Mac says, all yours. I stare at the gasping man, a few seconds before I know what I'm supposed to do. Mac is in from a second run with two dead men under his arms. He drops the corpses and heads back into the clearing. Come here you simple fuck Halverson shouts after him. Shit, Halverson chokes, what is this, what are we doing? Mac is hit, jerks upright, stumbles, keeps his balance and scoops up two more, both alive, his own blood seeping from somewhere above the elbow. Get your ass in here, Halverson shouts, you're bringing in dead guys. Get in here Mac, I say, you're hit, gotta take care of you. Mac blinks and his knees give way: he falls in a heap with the men he was carrying. Halverson and I belly crawl toward the wire to get him, barbs opening long streaks in my back as I go under and a direct hit scores the bunker just beyond, collapsing white light eaten by heat. Halverson goes to his knees for leverage and his right arm disappears, simply gone, hurricane wind. Blood's spuming out of the hole of his shoulder and he seems more surprised than hurt looking down at his blood spattering the mud. Mortar deafening, the long scream, earthquake crunch, volcanic explosion. Halverson stands up staring at his shoulder. Another direct hit lays down, cracking the night to empty out a primal roar, gravity reversed and gushing down and away, into the earth, into the belly of the earth, and something I don't see rushes into Halverson, folds him once, carries him oozing into mud thirty yards away.

The age at death is not a sign of value I tell the platoon's radioman. He nods and looks bewildered. A parrot lifts off above us. Tomorrow my life and times return to forest, in search of flames and snapshots to airmail home. I make suggestions that are nonsense: we all assume that life is short. I owe nothing to the form death takes.

When I speak it is for vain reasons.

II

I always choose the bunks on top and against the wall. Privacy. Vantage points. Due on duty in two hours. Another masked night flying for the dead. Texas and Rock howling about the wetback bitch they banged in Corpus Christi. Squadbay deserted except for us, nine o'clock Saturday night. Staring at waterpipe ten inches from my skull. Martha and the Vandellas on Armed Forces Radio. *Danger. Heartbreak Dead Ahead*. Jesus she squealed like a trapped rat when I gave it to her Texas roars. Opens another beer, yelling to me across the bunk tops You got any dope? Slide down and fish bag from my locker, walk to their table. Here, I say. Smoke your fuckin heads off.

Weird dude Texas says.

We stand on the runway in flight suits. Me with Rock. War makes us clairvoyant: two days before we watched Texas jog out to his chopper knowing somehow he was through, over, no more. Now we wait for the return of his remains. He was killed by a woman he tried to rape just south of Marble Mountain. Me and Rock on the runway, waiting. The pilot banks the helicopter to touch down and the engines stop, rotors slapping the air under their own power. Texas and the woman come off together. She small like you'd expect. Pretty in black. Handcuffed to Texas' stretcher. His body blanched but for the old blood where she stabbed him. Crewmen carry the stretcher past us and we turn to follow. In receiving the MPs unhook her. She looks up at me. She spits on me.

Helicopter approaching ground under fire: the earth seeming to flatten and recede, pulling back into its own daylight that we can see but not penetrate, everything in miniature, shadowed and working. Trees sway under the machine wind, distance leaving the ground fire hollow and artificial—random pops, stutters. Men run about, helmetless, gesturing and falling, comic if we did not know the situation, if we did not know what they were running from. The unit we are coming for has been caught in the open, retreating across a sunny flat toward a dike, taking casualties as we watch. There is a lurch in the air we pass and the earth roars suddenly toward us, trees and ground and running men surging into the vertical, gunfire slamming around our heads, smashing down from the placid sky we came out of. We take on men.

I am on the ground, loading: pushing, shoving, shouting. The other corpsmen start the fluids, bag breathe the near-dead, position men on stretchers and line them on the deck. No more than twenty feet away a marine is on the ground, writhing, calling out. I motion the crew chief to help me.

I am at the man's feet; we lift. My grip slips on his ankles: I catch at bootlaces and feel the pantlegs sag as if they are two bags filled with mud and it is everything I can do to keep a finger-grip on his laces and run forward. The chopper powers up. We are on board, lifting away. It is the sky again, the hovering silver border of the universe and my hands are shaking with their own memory of lifting those legs that were not legs, that had become something other than legs, that were glutinous mire, that were ooze, and we are in the sky and traveling the expanse of its silence, the open road of its vacant glory.

F ield hospital at night, a quiet moment never guaranteed simply by cover of darkness and I walk, up and back, restless amidst the sleep of the wounded, this sleight-of-hand version of sleep that crowds the air and resists the obvious visions, that tells the body nothing it has learned is true. I sit beside the lamp and look at the men triaged into positions along the tent wall, realizing that it is impossible to do a good job at war and expect to stay alive. To do his job a soldier gives up everything even when he believes he has not, signs over the roots of his life to a chain of command, a mandate, an initiative. It is always too late in the game when a soldier recognizes the depth of his sacrifice, too late then for anything other than dreaming — the last hope of recovery nested in the shape of any one man's life up to that point. Here, tonight, the tranced and half-conscious grapple with the void above their faces, crying out from time to time, a language in stunned reverse: the mirror-light of mirage. These are the stories of the names we have lost and there is a faith in dreams, a riding belief that no other instrument of regret might be so winsome, no other form of redress so sweetly hysterical. The reason is clear enough — in any random moment one's life might become suddenly and utterly unimportant beyond the number it is assigned, a life that becomes a citation, an enumerated article, purely of documentary and statistical value in the reports and dispatches and memorandums and cables and books of order, none of which can ever say the single true thing: *there are moments a man can be who he is a second time.* Alive when he thought he would never be alive again.

4 A.M. My relief comes in, dazed by the wake-up. He carries a worn deck of cards and a crushed half-pack of cigarettes. He motions his head toward the dark of the doorway. They got coffee in the mess tent, he says. If you can stand to drink it.

I dream about two Vietnamese monks. It is a desert and one of them is lame, the other blind. They live together and take care of one another's needs. When I encounter them I am in uniform, in jungle utilities. They take me in, feed me, but neither speaks. As time passes in their hovel I want to speak of something that troubles me. I hold their silence until the desire to speak burns in me and I yell, my voice startling the dream: *Would you kill another being for food?*

Immediately but slowly and smoothly they become trees, the shapes of their bodies the shapes of trees, their feet taking root, their arms and heads branching and leafing and flowering endlessly.

It is pleasant to imagine an old man's death. Pleasant to imagine living that long.

Past eighty years of age perhaps, tired, but grateful for life's long pleasures, the love of family, the achievements of productive work. In those last days it seems likely there will be a garden. Pests will be bad. I will work hard and beat them at their own game, using sonic resonators and laser terminators — or whatever gardeners use in that distant future — turning the pests away from their sources of life, making their native jungle as inhospitable as I now help make these jungles I move through. I might look back on this war with equanimity — my war, our war — and even a lingering small measure of pride in the job well done and survived some sixty years earlier. When I am an old man there will be a Vietnamese-American in the United States Senate, my accountant and family doctor and neighborhood florist will all be Vietnamese-Americans. They will have been born in California. None of them will have ever been to Vietnam, or have any desire to go. They will be unclear as to the specifics of the war between my country and the country of their grandparents and great-grandparents. None of us will speak of this war, of course. I will have to get back to my garden in any event, and from there to my bed, knowing in some immutable way which year and month and day is my last, knowing that every man hopes for a world of his own making. We all imagine life will extend its favor in the natural course of events, that we will come at last to live in a place that is bright and simple and clean. This is our penitential desire. It is a reasonable desire, an admirable ambition, and not to be faulted. It is how time rides. It is the light by which we live and die.

What's the loneliest sound you ever heard, Corporal?

*Me?*

Yeah.

*The loneliest sound?*

Yeah. A thing you hear that makes you feel, you know, alone.

*What kind of sound do you mean?*

A train at night. The sound of a train whistle in the middle of the night, a train going by out there in the dark. I'd hear train whistles like that when I was a kid, on my grandparents' farm.

*Yeah?*

I'd hear that whistle and I'd ask myself, where's that train going?

*Disappearing out there, I guess.*

Like it was going right up into the sky, climbing right up into the night.

*You ever wish you were on that train?*

I wish I was on it right now. I really do.

III

War stories are the oldest stories. The only truth left is the oblique moment, the casually turned head, the single look that is what we mean. Life to death is too short, too fast, out of nothing to this moment that is everything: the last night in-country and I dream of horsemen in smoking hills, shadows on horseback, reed breastplates, quirts, half-breed moon. Some other war. Some other ancient war but this same place, this same unspeakably beautiful place. Annam. Cochin China. Nam Viet, Viet Nam, and I am awake, standing among the other sleepers. The nightwatch drowses on a stool. I walk out into the dark's soft dense heat and piss on a bush, flushing something alive. Bird, rat. Look up into a coast of stars. Halverson had been angry with me when I told him the sun was a star. You lying sack of shit, he said, the sun is the goddam sun, that's all. Right, I told him, whatever. Looking up in the hour before dawn at the myriad suns of night in the sky over Asia, thinking that it is over. It's over. *You made it.* You made it.

Let us pray the Chaplain says over the plane's intercom. Lord we thank you for bringing these boys back to their loved ones in safety, for guarding over them in their times of duress and anguish, and for giving them the strength to serve their country and their God with selfless valor. We thank you for loving them in their moments of doubt, and for bearing away to your own grace those who you've plucked from their midst. We welcome them home and know that you do as well. Amen.

Maldonado only started praying when he knew help was coming, that we'd get out of the ditch. By then he'd lost too much blood, he was faint, listing toward shock, whispering for Jesus to help him. His lips moving when we slid him up out of the mud, the crucifix in his fist. The Chaplain eases down the aisle, touching men on the shoulder, shaking hands, his face florid, alcoholic, and I turn to the window to avoid him, feeling the cloud cover hum below as he passes. Let us pray. Let us pray, yes indeed, let us bow our heads, let us raise our voices in a consummate union, let our prayers rise to the surface of this ocean we cross. Take every man, woman, and child this war has killed and bless them as our offerings to ourselves, the never-ending body we spend to engage the terror of our emptiness. Take these dead men, women, children, and bless them, remember them without names, without histories, without songs. This is our entreaty and it is offered in the spirit of Xerox, Coca-Cola, General Electric, General Motors, Weyerhauser, Allied Chemical, in the spirit of Dresden and Hiroshima and Nagasaki and My Lai, in the spirit of every drowning ghost and airborne soul, amen.

Home from the war. Turning small, tight circles in the airport's blazing white, travelers swimming around the confused island of my body as I stare up at the clocks, at the arrival/departure boards, the back-lit man-high advertisements, past the suspended models of fighter planes from World War I and World War II and Korea and up, to the lights themselves, the lights imitating themselves, twenty-four hours a day the airport's private and distant ecstasy: a built-in heaven.

Reassigned to hospital duty to wait out my enlistment, and I feel as if I have no idea where I am. Only that it is not where I was. I pretend to be on specified duties as I wander the floors and grounds. On the fourth floor is a man who lost his bladder to a shrapnel fragment; he wears a plastic bag tied to his waist by a brocade cord. He cheerfully empties the bag twice daily. On the second floor is a man with both legs gone. He operates the hospital's basement games of chance and has made over thirteen thousand dollars in five months. He has no idea why he is still here but has no desire to leave. A sailor missing half his face has transferred to the psychiatric unit to avoid discharge. There is a man on the sixth floor who happened to be too near a Claymore mine on a particularly bad day, when he lost his right foot, testicles, and penis. A bald priest visits this hospital which is in his parish, extending the warm greetings of the Holy Trinity. I stand alone at windows watching the Pacific's sheen, pelicans slicing out of the sun. It is the bright calm of North America, the coast of California, the city of San Francisco: arbored streets and hillside parks and the laughter of children, a broad and open light.

There was a time when I kept thinking of floating over a planet and being sucked into its face, like watching a kiss coming. I remember, once before leaving a helicopter the crew chief said They won't have time to turn around twice out there. He didn't think anybody heard him. I don't know why I did. That night I tried to sleep on an ammo chest in one of the harshest storms we knew, assuming it was my last mission. Now I pass time, unaccounted for. In the emergency room I see a black girl with blood on her face, surrounded by white coats. I ride the elevator thinking of swimming in the bay below the hospital, imagining its water might domesticate my skin. Once, I remind myself, I had wanted to say something true about love.

B us to the downtown terminal, AWOL from the hospital and still in uniform. Cross the street and step over a chain into a parking lot where two overweight whores argue with a man in a yellow hat with white feathers, the three huddled beside a pink Chrysler Imperial. The engine's running, radio up inside the car: Four Tops. *Sugar pie honey bunch. Don't you know that I love you?*

Beyond the parking lot The House of Joy, Cupid's Corner, Vixen's, the Adonis Film Club, neon humming and rippling at one-thirty in the afternoon. Walking toward Market Street, a man in an American Legion hat stops me. He's wearing sunglasses that reflect my face back to me: he nods and extends his hand. Welcome home son he says. All I can see in his face is my face, cautious and older, looking at me as if I'm a stranger. I don't know you I say.

The Strand Theatre, an old man trussed in an ancient coat and tie inside the smeared box office. Three movies for a dollar and the old man creaks forward with a ticket ripped from a yellow roll.

The theatre's nearly empty, somebody toward the back smoking reefer. I sit midway down, the movie in progress with Jack Webb in the title role as a marine drill sergeant with redeeming qualities. The scene is emotional, Webb in dress blues at a bar, filled with regret.

I dream heavily, faces washing out or blowing off like leaves edging out of season, singers muted by whatever it is they know but won't tell me. Now I'm following, calling for them to wait. They turn a corner and I'm alone until they emerge somewhere behind me. I turn back to find them and wake with a start, lace of marijuana still in the theatre. I blink into the screen's light, stiff-necked. Another movie and Steve McQueen looks to be sixteen: he's talking about how The Blob is going to eat the whole country. Maybe even the world.

I tried to write letters home. I wanted to talk about what I saw and felt, what it tasted like, the unfortunate things I had learned about human beings. Most of my letters went unfinished. Plain truth seemed fantastic, frankly unbelievable. Or simply brutal without good reasons. Everybody's life, I told myself, was hard enough already; they had no need to hear how I spent the last years of my boyhood, high-strung with weaponry in a distant jungle. I knew that after the war nothing in my life would feel true for a long time to come, except perhaps my imagination, the private life my imagination might carry, aside from me, beyond me. I was convinced that, in the end, nothing could be explained unless I talked about the smell of rain at night, or the sight of a farmer's face before his pig flock was mutilated by machine-gun fire, or the single glance into the doorway of a thatch-blaze when I saw the figure inside moving and on fire and knew it was too late, too late, always too late.

Strung up by a hind leg on a
vanquished year, wind stiff around my neck
and disappearing up there in the leaves.
Never thought I'd feel old
but that's the chance you take, blowing
the pipes clear, the one clean line
burning your hands.
Blood under the bridge.
Forget it someone says, touching my shoulder.
You're home now.
It's springtime.

Richard Currey is a two-time recipient of NEA fellowships, in both poetry and fiction. He is most recently the author of *The Wars of Heaven*, a short-story collection that includes winners of both the O. Henry and Pushcart Prizes. His novel, *Fatal Light*, cited by Tim O'Brien as "one of the very best works of fiction to emerge from the Vietnam war," has appeared in ten languages and won the Special Citation of the Hemingway Foundation and the Vietnam Veterans of America's Excellence in the Arts Award.

Cover design by Anne Garner.
The cover watercolor, *Red Poppy #2*, and the etchings on page ii (*The Orchard*) and page 61 (*Poppy Landscape*) are by Art Hansen.
Book design by Stacy Feldmann and Jamie Potenberg.
Composed in Centaur by Wilsted & Taylor, Oakland.
Printed by Braun-Brumfield, Ann Arbor.